BEYOND THE MARGINS

An Autism Journey Through Poetry

Rey Adira

Fractal Landscape

CONTENTS

Preface

I think the writings you will find here in the beginning are my desperate attempts to make sense of myself, who I am, how I think and operate and why it does not seem to sync up with the rest of the world – all pre ASD diagnosis. There is much angst around the search and the struggle to understand the "why". Something I have learned is common trait of Autists. I know I am different and the way I perceive the world seems very different from others. I am searching to understand my inability to really connect with others. It's such a struggle. An attempt to understand the exterior world – which seems so foreign to me. Nature makes sense to me – the world we have created as humans, does not. It is my assumption that many people may experience these struggles, and I have no idea if my ASD exacerbated this or how it impacted this process at all. But I can say from the inside looking out, the way others seemed to experience the world was so dissimilar to the way I was experiencing it. Looking back, I know I was, and remain, incredibly sensitive to the world and the actions of others. I have no filter which makes even the day-to-day confusing and often overwhelming.

CHAPTER 1: SEARCHING

Unknown

I am searching. I search everywhere I go. I search endlessly, everywhere within everything I see. I search in other people, in my surroundings, in society in other cultures. I search within myself. I search my heart, my mind, my soul. I know not what I am searching for. Is it peace, tranquility? Is it love or feeling? Is it knowledge or divine inspiration. Am I searching for freedom from boundaries I am unable to see? Chains that forever hold me in place. Something to fill this void. The deepest of caverns, hollow, dark, empty, cold. Anything to stop this relentless wind that whips through my soul in search of passage out and away. The wind cuts and its thunderous voice overwhelms my independent thought and drowns my cries for help. I am lost.

But if I found what I am searching for, would I know? Would I be capable of harnessing such limitless energy in pure form? Or would I just bend to the whims of the winds as a tree bends to a gale force wind?

I long to flow. I long to flow effortlessly as a leaf blows in a warm, gentle springtime breeze. To tumble as the brook upon the stones. No understanding, no resistance, just flowing; carried along at the whims of nature herself. But even the brook eventually ends up in the vast expansion of the ocean to be carried by the tides. A sea full of multitudinous desires. Shifting back and forth under lunar influence.

I long to feel. I long to exist, not only within myself, but out there. I long to innervate life as a nerve ending innervates the muscle fibers within the body. To be a part of the whole. I search so diligently. I think if only I can get more education, more knowledge, I will have it. But what I long for is not found in the confines of higher education. It is somewhere. I sense it. But the more I reach out, the further it pulls away. The harder I search, the more difficult it becomes to find. The interminable question: Do I know what I believe, or do I just believe what I think I know?

I long to be free. Not oppressed by societal and historical beliefs. Not confined by this world or the physicality of it. A glass box. I live within a glass box. I can see the world out there, but when I reach for it, my hand is deflected away. Sometimes I run hard into the glass, trying to shatter it, my perceptions. I think if I can perceive the box as just chemical and physical properties, I can break through. My mind, the void., the darkness. The sun is scorching outside the glass box. I am suffocating within. The heat holds me at bay. The glass box is all I know, my prison without bars.

I long to fear. To cry at the sound of whispers on the wind. What would they tell me? To shudder at the thunder as it booms so omnipotently around me. To cower at the first flash of lightening. To fear what man desires to control. Such power, such energy. I fear. I fear but I am not allowed to show it in this glass box; for it is supposed to protect me. Funny how I don't feel safe. I feel trapped. My animal instincts sometimes overcome me, and I am plagued with the desire to break free. Nothing else to occupy my mind. The fear is overwhelming. I want to cry, to run away. But I am still within my glass box.

The translucence is maddening. I keep running and running Into these boundaries I cannot see. I am black and blue. There is no respite. I want to drift aimlessly, as the white clouds drift above me in the limitless sky, continuously changing shape, changing form. The sky, endless, infinite in every direction I turn. I want my mind to be free, endless as the sky. No more of what they tell me is important to know. No more boundaries.

But alas, I will withdraw within my glass walls. I will not push the boundaries of this world, of my world. I will remain within the confines of my glass box withering away. My soul will forever continue the search. For my soul longs for an answer, my soul longs to be free.

Madness

The madness is blinding
Roads are winding
Bells ringing
Children singing
Animals dying
Babies crying
Universe expanding
Aliens landing
Crime growing
Preacher's sowing
Trees falling
Mother Earth calling
Poverty stricken
Politicians sicken
Rage overtaking
War in the making
Diseases spreading
Death's heading
Greed overrunning
Selfishly cunning
Hate bearing
Love sparing
The road is winding
The madness is blinding

Searching By Moonlight

Through the insatiable darkness
Through the night of no end
The path continues onward
With no warning as it curves and bends

Moonlight of sanity
Grows ever more dim
Swallowed by dark, foreboding clouds
I am no longer what I had been

But was I ever anything
That could be defined
Or has this journey
Completely overtaken my mind

Cold and alone
I press forward on this trip
There is no going back
For death comes with just one slip

I must remain fully aware
Crawling now on hands and knees
The fear weighs heavily
Fear of something I cannot see

And the fear alone
Would be reason enough to pause
As the elements close in
I fall victim to nature's laws

Yet who am I to defy
Boundaries holding me at bay
Am I strong enough to break through the darkness
And reach the mystical light of day

Hubris

Wind whispered secrets
Natures story to unfold,
Life full of wonder,
Who are we to be so bold.

Mass destruction at our fingertips,
Illusions of control.
Information highway,
Leaving us bereft of any soul.

Are we a god given blessing,
Or evolutions plan.
Knowledge is power,
Or could it be the fall of man?

We Do Not Come In Peace

Plague of the earth
We do not come in peace
Conquer and exploit
Dominion over the beasts

Money and power
So often sought
Illusions of control
Can be traded and bought

Eight billion strong
Death be not near
Science will save us
From all that we fear

Acres a minute
Fall at our touch
Mother earth beware
It will never be enough.

Population number updated

Alexthymia (Updated Title)

I have spent so long inside myself
Trying desperately to understand
Feelings and emotions
That have long since been out of hand

And I wonder what it must be like
Out there in the realm of the living
Where people just seem to float along
Unaware of what they are giving

This knowing that fills my heart and soul
Seem such a part of what I am
I don't want to live unknowingly
Going through life without giving a damn

But this path seems so much more painful
A daily struggle just to survive
I may carry the world on my shoulders
But at least I know I am alive

National Rifle Association

They keep telling us
That everything will be okay
The politicians, the analyst
The NRA

But then one kid shoots another
And it makes the tv
Giving another kid the idea
To screw the powers that be

Politicians go to war
Still change does not come
Lobbyists alter the score
While no one tallies the sum

And the sum of all
Equals children are dying
While capitol hill is fighting battles
Parents continue crying

Still, some spout the constitution
Bearing arms is a god given right
We must protect ourselves they say
From impending violence in the night

But who will protect the children
From the bullet with no name
We all bear responsibility
For allowing society's shame

Depression

The fury within
Rages eternal
Doubts created
By demons infernal

The silence pervades
Dark clouds loom
Skies unleash
An inevitable doom

The void surrounds
Time stands still
Chaos ensues
A battle of will

The nothing envelopes
Emptiness prevails
Reaching inside
Into depths of hell

Life

Turn myself inside out
To find what is real
Cold and exposed
Trapped where time stands still

What I thought was truth
Was elaborate deception
Faith destroyed
By evils' inception

Innocence lost
Perspective shift
Dark views control
Visions lost in the mist

Sanity wavers
Emotions ebb and flow
Chaos unleashed
Embracing the soul

Gaia

She silently watches
As trees come down
As air becomes unbreathable
And toxic waste poisons the ground

She is unobtrusively aware
Of green paper exchanging hands
Of the explosion of a species
Which makes a commodity of her lands

She humbly observes
As ice caps melt
And water becomes polluted
While she suppresses the rage she has felt

When she speaks
She will speak multitudes
To remind us of the powerlessness of man
How in reality we are inconsequential
To the universes ultimate plan

Seeking

Silence speaks eternal
Messages to the soul
Finality of existence
More pieces of the whole
Questions to be answered
Purpose to be sought
Desire to frustration
Reason cannot be bought

Conflicted

Life full of mystery
Who are we to unravel
Encoded secrets
Still, we continue to dabble

Endless pursuit of knowledge
While emptiness prevails
To fill our need temporarily
Discount stores offer 24-hour sales

And preachers cry from the pulpit
"We are in a state of moral decay"
"We must stand up and be heard"
"To make sure our beliefs all must obey'

Division continues to grow
Fueled by ignorance and fear
Labels become walls
As battle lines draw near

Some turn to religion
For their arsenal of defense
While others turn to science
Depending on logic and measured sense

But both seem to have forgotten
That the complexity of life
Should be valued and honored
Not simplified or spliced.

Adulting

Walls of conformity
Are swiftly closing in
Trapped by shades of ideology
Where all colors blend

Such ever present longing
Desire to be free
To break through the boundaries
Integrated into me

Overwhelm

Often the pain is so intense
And the fear so blindly overwhelms
I am left in a nightmare reality
Where I am no longer at the helm

A place where the vortex surrounds me
And all else has been destroyed
Through the darkness lies desolation
All my defenses have been deployed

Strange how in this darkness
That seems to absorb all light
The pain feels less severe
For I can withdraw into the night

Where there is nothing left to do but wait
For there is no place left to hide
The chaos and fury will come
And I will be swept away in the emotional tide

Shutdown (Updated Title)

Impenetrable void
Hidden deeply within
Drained of life not lived
Back to where I have been

Tired and alone
Fear holds me at bay
Safest place to be
Away from the light of day

Emptiness prevails
As loneliness consumes
Lost in the void never seen
Trapped in my own silent tomb

The Path Of Most Resistance

I walk along the edge of reality
Where chaos and order intertwine
Where dawn and dusk are inseparable
Where consciousness enters mind.

A place where time and space are disjointed
Yet the connections are pervasive and clear
Where truth become deception
And the futility of life is ever near.

I tread lightly on this path
For few have been here before
The way often treacherous and lonely
Yet the allure consistently tugs at my core

The knowledge needed to maneuver
And the compass used to direct
Found deep in the recesses of my spirit
For it is there I feel the effect

And though few may journey with me
In this reality of turmoil and pain
This path will lead me to heights
Thought by most impossible to attain

Snowflake

I once knew a cat names Snowflake
Who belonged to the people next door
But Snowflake truly belonged to no one
For Snowflake was feral to the core

The people must not have taken much care
For Snowflake was always on guard
Walking over our cars crying for attention
And stalking poor little creatures in our yard

And every once in awhile
Snowflake would make a kill
Then drop it proudly at my feet
Looking to me to approve her feline will

This was not always easy
Sometimes these creatures were still in pain
Snowflake would slowly terrorize them
For to her, they were just a game

Over the years I grew to love Snowflake
For it was only then I began to understand
This behavior was inherent to her nature
Despite the attempted domestication by man.

CHAPTER 2: CHANGE

This next set of poems and writings are expressing the inevitable change that is about happen. I am about to graduate from Graduate School and have already begun looking for jobs in an academic setting. Change is difficult for me. Small changes are difficult enough – but major changes such as this can be so overwhelming and of course, at the time, I was unaware why change was so very difficult for me to process. I had literally been in school beginning in $4^{y/o}$ Kindergarten up to High School and then 12 more years of post-secondary education. Academia was my comfort zone and as I look back on my experiences there – school was a struggle. Not the learning part – it was the social aspects that made school so very difficult for me. The social politics. People were the problem, not the content of what I was learning. I remember in 3rd grade when my mother would pick my sister and me up from school – I would often fall into the backseat of the car with a migraine headache that lasted the rest of the afternoon and evening. It was life that was difficult. I loved to learn and still do. I was fortunate enough to be able to assimilate well enough to make it through school and it provided some structure but also allowed for the flexibility I need as well to thrive, plus my incessant desire to learn. Being a student was easy – being a person in society was not. And now I was going to have to leave my comfort zone and transition out into the big, scary world fraught with political and social mine fields. Not that I didn't experience some of that in school as well. In fact, that was the most difficult aspect of all of my schooling - politics.

Dead Zone

I am too far away
To lead me to myself.
Trapped in crowded spaces
I have placed on a shelf.

Feelings I have buried
So that I might survive.
I must now unearth
To know I am alive.

Illusion

Memories are only visions
Somehow trapped in time
The only way they exist
Is if you replay them in your mind

They have no bearing on the present
For they are just snapshots of the past
Each version plays out differently
Depending upon the member of the cast

And sometimes it makes me wonder
This concept of what is real
If ever given the chance
Would I take the red or the blue pill?

For if the past is only a memory
And memories are little more than dreams
Then it all would be an illusion
And nothing is as it seems

If

If I found myself
Then who would I be?
Can I live with no boundaries
In such a well-defined society?

If I free my mind,
Of what I think I know.
Would the chains fall away
Giving my soul room to grow?

If I had no desire,
And no need to control,
Could I find the peace
So long the elusive goal?

Ephemeral

Clouds so immense
In their impermanent glory
To look away and back again
Each time they tell a different story

If only to float among them
With no need of control
To change with every heartbeat
An infinite reshaping of the soul

Optimism

Whispers on the wind,
Awaken me from my slumber.
A life pulsating from within,
Beat of a different drummer.

A new day unfolds,
As I rise for a better view.
Distant horizon shadowed,
By mountain peaks I once knew.

The path laid out before me,
Seems unfamiliar and overgrown.
As if when I take the first step,
I will be the only this path has ever known.

Within

Is there a truth
Our fragile minds might ask.
A reality undiscovered
Just beyond our grasp.

Something so infinitely subtle,
Yet greater than ourselves.
A vastness undefined,
Timeless essence that prevails.

Is there any truth,
Our unconscious would know.
Recognizable not by senses,
Hidden deep within the soul.

The final frontier of exploration,
To ultimately look within.
And there might truth be found,
Where understanding begins.

Truth

Trapped by the illusion
Of whom I am supposed to be
Lost in the conflict
Of a never-ending duality

Overwhelmed by emotions
I can no longer control
Frightened by a truth
Breeching the depths of my soul

Driven by a longing
Very few understand
Conscious of a reality
Moving beyond times sand

Searching for the answers
So that I might be free
Discovering different pieces
That make the puzzle of me

Change

Navigating the waters
Of consciousness and time
Lured by voices
Speaking only in my mind

Following a vision
Seemingly so unclear
Caught in a vortex
Of all that I fear

Weary of this battle
Between me and myself
Searching for answers
Between pages on a shelf

Strengthened by the insight
The journey has just begun
Many oceans left to cross
Sailing into the rising sun

CHAPTER 3:
ASSIMILATION

I am now in my first career position, where it matters as far as building a career. Looking back, the toll this takes on me is astounding and it is a wonder I survived. The political machinations of others are still difficult for me to understand and tolerate. Systems become the problem and the people who run those systems. I know I am sensing I am being devoured by the system and am losing myself to it. I see this as certain death. So, I begin to withdraw from myself to survive. Now that I know the enormous amount of masking this took, I can understand my fatigue and exhaustion as the years progress.

Disappear

She ran to the forest, her inner voice guiding her way. She could constantly sense the silent, invisible tendrils reaching towards her, pulling her towards this mysterious place. So she went, floating along as if in a dream. And there, on the fringe, she briefly hesitated, looking around to see what she would be leaving behind. It took only a moment for her to take stock knowing it would be only a vague memory when she crossed that boundary into the unknown.

The smell of cedar and fir was overwhelming at first, intertwined with the pungent odor of decay. The large branches only allowing intermittent rays of light to filter through as she tentatively moved deeper into the womb. The mist surrounded her as she moved forward letting her heart guide her through the dense foliage. Had she relied on her physical senses, she would have surely been lost for they had become obsolete. Her eyes told her everything looked the same in every direction she turned. Her ears heard only the sounds of silence and her own pounding heartbeat. Her skin was clammy from the never-ending mist enshrouding her keeping her surprisingly warm. The smell of life mixed with death was pervasive. She soon realized she must let go of her old ways of sensing her reality and only then she began becoming truly aware of this strange, new place. As if she was awakened from a deep sleep, she could see for the first time the intricacy of life and the necessity of death. The wheel as it spins round and round. The interconnection, the very fabric of time.

She began to hear the almost imperceptible sounds that surrounded her, that had always surrounded her. The silence of peace. She felt the light breeze as it stirred ever so softly, and she smelled the smell of all life and all death. Last to come to her was the sense of taste. A taste of untreated, pure water from an underground spring. A spring so clear it could have been pouring from the very essence of life itself. She drank deeply, as if she had never tasted anything so pure in her life. And she hadn't. Here, she discovered a whole new reality. She allowed these newly developed senses to guide her through the unfamiliar. So difficult, yet the forest leant her some of its ancient wisdom. She would have been frightened to go it alone.

Her quest was not complete however until she moved deeply enough into this now, strange but somehow enticingly familiar place. Until she became one with it. With all life, until she was no more.

Lost

I am lost. Lost in a jungle of nothingness. I no longer recognize my surroundings for everything is beginning to look the same. I no longer recognize myself and I feel disjointed and disconnected. The path I once walked so assuredly has been absorbed by the nothingness. And I am forced to walk aimlessly without any sense of direction. I fear. I fear that I too will be engulfed by this nothing, this black hole from which not even light can escape. The event horizon grows ever closer. I can sense its presence, and I know of its power.

There was no fight, no battle for it had surrounded me before I was even aware of its intention. My world was gone and in its place was this nothing. This lifeless, barren, wasteland of no purpose, no direction. It is taking all my strength just to keep moving so that it cannot fully consume me as it has my world. I fear if I stop, I too will disappear. Yet there is nowhere left for me to go. The impending nothing is encroaching upon my very soul and I long to slide into its abysmal embrace. To succumb to its power, surrender to the inevitable, to be found in the nothing.

Inward I Go

I sit and ponder the darkness
The absence of all light
Wondering what mysteries it might behold
As I gaze into the night.

And in the stillness and solitude
There is a dreaded embrace
Of all the unknowing and uncertainty
And all that I fear to face.

For maybe in this impenetrable blackness
Where I can no longer see past myself
Must I finally be forced to look inward
And acknowledge all with which I have not dealt.

For this must be why I fear the darkness
Representing all I must overcome
With the knowledge it will always be there
Just the other side of the sun.

Revisiting

I am losing my perspective
In these ever-shifting sands
Trapped in a wasteland of nothingness
Overwhelmed by the emptiness of these lands

And I am lost in the void of isolation
Where time and space are the same
Still, it seems vaguely familiar
As if I should know it by name

And it is almost as though I have been here
Perhaps many times before
Only subtle differences disorient me
Leaving a new terrain to explore

Still there is a sense of trepidation
For am unsure which direction to go
But alas, I must put one foot forward
And begin this journey only I can know

Winds Of Change

Winds of change blow steadily
Bending me to its desires
So often have I resisted
Finding it is only myself that tires.

And it is the fear that wears me so
A stiffness in my soul
The unwillingness to surrender
To the winds mentoring role

Although these changes do lead in new directions
Paths different from others I have known
The winds have never led me astray
For it is only through change that I have grown

Complete Overwhelm

I speak only in silence
My soul crying for release
Lost in a world of shadows
In this struggle to find peace.

I dare not speak of the pain
Or well of darkness that overflows
Seeping into the void
The hollowness no one else knows.

How often I fear I cannot survive
As the battle rages on
Too brief a victory
Awakening to the light of dawn.

Still, something in me presses forward
Despite the agony and fear
For I will not call for a retreat
Although the darkness surges ever near

Search For Freedom

Take this pain,
I can no longer bear.
The loneliness,
I am too weary to wear.

Strip me down,
Till I am naked and exposed.
Weight of the world a burden,
Crushing me unopposed.

Silence this chorus of voices,
Echoing in my head.
Speaking to me of paths,
I no longer tread.

Free me from this vessel,
Of binding flesh and bone.
Allowing my soul the freedom,
To find its own way home.

Destiny

A pattern in the chaos
Underlying order we cannot see.
Purpose we cannot define
Logic to reality.

A future we cannot know
Variations of time and chance
Designed fate versus free will
Statistics of circumstance.

Still a yearning to understand
That which is greater than ourselves
The science of god
Unanswered questions prevail.

Overwhelming Loss

There is a truth I must tell
The story of the trees
If we would stop and listen
Such wisdom would bring us to our knees.

For these ancient ones hold such power
A serenity none can define
Secrets left untold
Because tales take too much time

But often when I am among them
There is a sense of humility and awe
Their understanding so complete
Their silent contemplation unflawed

So, when I see these gentle giants
Brutally cut to their knees
I weep in silent mourning
For the loss of the wisdom of the trees.

Environmental Discourse

Forgive us our trespasses
For we know not what we do
An ignorant and greedy species
Myopic in our view.

Failing to understand the concepts
The wonder in evolutions design
The interdependence of all life
True nature of the divine.

For we think of nothing but profit
In a reality created by man
Egocentric in our actions
A plague upon the land.

Forgive us our trespasses
For we know not what we do
Nothing will remain
Before we are through.

Conforming

I am both lost and found
Unable to utter a sound.
As the world passes me by
I look inward where answers lie.

Still, I cannot seem to find my way
Knowing my perceptions keep me at bay.
Trapped by walls I cannot see
Living a lie of conformity.

"The Truth Is Out There"

Buried within this chaos
Lies the order of the divine
Complex in its interweaving
Simplistic in its design

To most it is intangible
Though our subconscious is ultimately aware
Hidden deeply within the visible
Blinding us with its glare

And it is "the question that drives us"
Seeking that which cannot be found
To break free from the reality
This darkness to which I am bound

For the "truth must surely be out there"
And will certainly set us free
If only to see past the illusions
That so define my boundary

Assimilation

Leaves rustle softly beneath her feet. A silent breeze blows evidenced only by her sense of touch and the trees swaying gently around her. She stops suddenly and breathes deeply as if she is breathing life into the void that has consumed her for so long.

A river rages violently to her right. One of many conveying the lifeblood of all from the seasonal snow melt resting within the giant, craggy peaks overshadowing her presence.

She is perishing. Slowly, ever so slowly she is being crushed by the terrible weight of life. A burden that has never lifted and has left her empty and exhausted. There is no respite, no recourse.

She wants to run. Run to escape what was, what is. Run toward the possibility. If only to run free. To release the seeds of distrust she must carry regarding other's intentions. To shed the skin of armor she has been forced to don for her own protection. To escape the endless machinations and greedy ambitions of others of her kind. If only to run free. The lightness of being carrying her every step. To run freely through the meadows with mountain peaks sheltering her from the storms. To explore the unknown of the dark, mysterious forest. To delight in the rainbow of color found in each sun-stricken water droplet.

She seeks the solace, the solitude. She will not last much longer in her world. She must escape and begin the process of disarmament. If she remains, there will be little left that is recognizable, and she will surely fall prey to the chaos and depravity.

Embrace

Dark, grey clouds loom large on the horizon
A winter's landscape permeates my view
Such obsolete silence overwhelms
Death providing for life anew.

I wonder how long I have been here
In this barren land I have sought
I wonder how long I must remain
In this reality where time is caught.

For surely there must be a reason
My journey has led me to this place
A quiet time of reflection
A darkness I must embrace.

Lottery Of Life

We search for some sense of meaning
Purpose we can somehow call our own
Reason for our suffering and sorrow
Means to control the unknown.

We turn to god for the answers
Looking for someone to thank or blame
An omnipotent, omniscient being
Dolling out both tragedy and mercy in his name.

But ultimately the question still lingers
For there is randomness we cannot understand
Life is either one great lottery
Or god deals cards with a loaded hand.

Gasping For Air

I struggle against this current
Deceptive undertow pulling me down
An ocean of chaos and confusion
This battle to which I am bound.

Swelling tides crash against my body
Cold depths seep at my soul
I fear I am falling to shadow
Raging surge taking its toll.

Limbs grow ever more weary
As I fight for one final breath
Weight of the world on my shoulders
Carrying me to my death

Death Becomes Her

Thoughts shrouded in mystery
This wreck I have become
Lost in never ending conflict
Where parts do not equal the sum.

Struggles seem to intensify
I fear I am losing my grip
No longer able to process
From reality I begin to slip.

Pain becomes unbearable
And I suffocate with each breath
Darkness seeps into my soul
Bringing the gentle embrace of death.

Burial

Fragments of a broken past
Lie strewn throughout my mind
Shards of buried memory
Thought better left behind.

Disjointed figures beckon
Remains of paths once tread
Fractured time and space reveal
Lessons of lives once lead.

Shattered images reflect
Little of me remains
Can what was lost, now be found
Along this path of pain.

At this point in my life – I am as assimilated as I will become, and I completely shut down and have shut out the rest of the world. I guess I go into survival mode. I won't write again for 15 years. I am moving forward in my career – completely bereft of any emotions – empty. I often think of these years as my "Data" years – the android from Star Trek the Next Generation. All head and 100% masking – completely shut down and I have shut the world out. This is the only way I can survive the world. When I can no longer mask and protect myself, the emotions do return, and they return with a vengeance.

Late 2019

In late 2019 – still pre-ASD diagnosis; I watched a documentary on the practice of Shark Finning. I was so overwhelmed by what I saw I wrote these next words in about 5 minutes. Perhaps this is what started the process of my return to myself?

I woke in the night
From a most horrific dream
Filled with monsters and villains
And nightmarish things.
I checked under the bed
All the closets and my shed
Seeking the monster
That had brought me such dread.
I glanced in the mirror
To assure my fragile mind
What reflected back
Was the only monster I could find.

World On Fire

In October 2020, during the COVID lockdowns, the pacific northwest region experienced about 7-9 straight days of air quality that was so poor – it was unsafe to breathe the air. You couldn't go outside some days. You couldn't see to drive. Couldn't see 3 feet out the window. It was a surreal and poignant experience. A warning of what is to come, if only we paid attention. Parts of California, Oregon, Washington and British Columbia were burning and it converged and descended over parts of Washington state.

Awoke in the morning
To an apocalyptic sight
Red smoke and haze
Blocking all-natural light.

The many who are suffering
Yet we feel no shame
We deflect, dismiss, and dislodge
The truth we are to blame.

For a world on fire
Both in metaphor and fact
Callous indifference
With no will to act.

Instead, we post opinions
Based on fiction and lies
Wrapping ourselves in bubbles
While the planet around us dies.

CHAPTER 4: BREAKDOWN

Early September of 2021, I began to struggle with my energy, my ability to think, to function on a day-to-day basis. I was easily angered; my emotions were all over the map and I could not manage them or my thoughts at all. I couldn't focus to complete even basic tasks. The thought of going online and paying a bill was just too much. The mail would pile up on my table and I couldn't even open it. If my spouse asked me to do anything extra, I would either explode or break down. It was like a crash. I went from very high functioning to basically non functioning capacity. I couldn't even think, much less act or "do". About 4 weeks into that, I decided I might need some help. I found a therapist who initially diagnosed me with Generalized Anxiety Disorder. But after a couple of weeks of therapy and getting a better handle on my history and me – she asked if I had ever been diagnosed with ASD. Of course, I had not. I was familiar enough from movies and tv shows, but that was the extent of my knowledge base around it. After a series of tests and assessments, turns out, I was ASD Level 1 and what I was experiencing was referred to as Autistic Burnout. This happens when someone has been masking for so long, and so much, they literally "crash" and can no longer continue to mask or function at a high level. After doing some of my own research on ASD, my life began to make sense. Now came the healing and the process of learning to unmask. A process of self-discovery and acceptance. Something I am still working on today. If you have had to be someone else, just to survive the world for 51 years- how do you even begin to peel that back and really know who you are? How do you shed a mask that has kept you safe and allowed you to "fit in" to a world you do not understand and that completely overwhelms you?

Regret

Long have I sought the answers
The quest lonely, the path unknown
A life of solitude and reflection
An epic journey undertaken alone.

Often the path is difficult
Storms rage with no shelter in sight
Fatigue and weariness set in
Still, I must continue at first light.

The enemy remains elusive
Understanding and knowledge key
A lifelong effort in pursuit
In hopes of finding me.

Resistance

Within these prison walls
A child lonely and confused
Trapped in the essence of time
Lost, neglected, abused.

Elaborate scaffolding surrounds
Persona exemplified
Protects the lonely child
From the dangers of the wild.

Masks designed to accommodate
The nature of life itself
Meaning, interpretation, and purpose
Sought in books on a shelf.

Ever vigilant and alone
These thoughts bind me here
Feelings submerged in darkness
Lost in a sea of fear.

There is no route to escape
Still, the child longs to flee
This child I would destroy
If you tried to set them free.

Life- Part 1

Life full of wonder
Full of amazing and beautiful things
Boundless and unstoppable
Still in death the toll bell rings.

And mixed within the beauty
Chaos of pain and despair
Searching for purpose and meaning
While trapped in the cyclic snare.

For there is no way to escape
Both pleasure and pain
Finite tragedy of existence
Reality, in name.

Life- Part 2

Life, a fleeting moment in time and space
Infinite, yet discrete, subject to universal grace
Nothing yet determined, or is it all fate
Trapped in the cycle, no way to escape.

Only death brings certain peace
Final chapter, freeing release
Yet a will to live pushes back
False hope, odds stacked.

"The quintessential human delusion"
A barrier few see past
Is there really something better
Or has the die already been cast?

Unknown

There is a part of me that's silent
A sadness pervasive and cruel
An emptiness unspoken
Survival the only rule.

Enveloped in blinding darkness
A never-ending night
Lost in a world disordered
Elusive is the light.

Loneliness seems eternal
Hopelessness consumes
Trapped by other's machinations
The monster forever looms.

Fear

The real fear is in knowing
The truth of what is to be
Both fate and circumstance
Conspire against what is me.

For there is a world unhindered
Free from loneliness and despair
But it's not my world
Mine traps me in its snare.

And although I long to escape
From my world, barren and vast
It is all I have ever known
The die long ago cast.

I understand the rules
Locked in its intricate maze
Isolated in my world
On my soul it preys.

Searching

To be or not to be
The various parts of me
If only to be free
From bonds I cannot see

Is it safe to be
If not, I can't agree
To follow the map of me
A journey I can't foresee

Can a life ever be
Exactly what we see
A life made of debris
The hidden reality

What does it mean to be
A question I agree
Imprisoned by decree
The monster within me

Misunderstood

Such burning desire
To be understood
Still always knowing
No one ever could

A life of confusion
Of sadness and sorrow
Emptiness and pain
Wake to tomorrow

Overwhelming
Intensity and fire
All the while
Walk a tight wire

Comfort at depths
Pressure would crush
Anyone
Who cared enough

Pervasive need to connect
Yet an inability to relate
Obtrusive frustration
Alone I wait

Heavy

There is no escape
From this cycle of pain
Where darkness and shadows
And demon's reign

Over and over
Battles are fought
Trenches appear
Scarring the heart

Soul grows weary
Barriers in place
Cycle continues
Losing the race

Walls crumble
Reality floods in
Pulling me under
Drowning again

Fighting to the surface
Drawing last breath
Weight of existence
Dragging me to my death

Echoes Of Me

There is a sorrow that burrows
Deep into my soul
An isolation and loneliness
In opposition to the role

A character played
Perfectly on script
When the lights are on
And the stage is equipped

But when the final applause fades
And the curtain falls
Emptiness returns
Leaving echoes in the halls

Undone

Can anyone even see
This chaos I have become
The battles in my head
Fictional heroes unsung

Imaginary friends
Fill my everyday
Providing a source of comfort
When reality gets in the way

Reality of a loneliness
A darkness in my soul
The burden too cumbersome
For one person to control
So I turn to fictional beings
Ones who understand
The ones holding me together
While my mind disbands

In the end
All that ever remains
Is the void of existence
And a heart that forever refrains

Who Would I Be

Sometimes, I don't want to be me
But who would I be
If I was not me?
Sometimes, I think, no one can see
How lonely and dark
These parts of me.
Sometimes I want to climb up a tree
Hidden away
No one can find me.
Sometimes, I think, I just want to be
Shedding the pain
This weight of me.
Sometimes, I feel, the need to be free
To be by myself
So I can just be.
Sometimes, I fear, what others might see
Allowing them in
To know the real me.
Sometimes, I think this isn't me
Ugly and scarred
Forever I'll be.
Sometimes I know, alone I will be
If anyone sees
The monster in me.

Timeless

Some days the world
Silently passes me by
Other days weighing heavily
On my soul to comply

A never ending battle
The space in between
Living up to standards
An elusive dream

Seemingly no respite
The pressure to be
Status of becoming
Whatever is me

Hidden

There is a large part of me
That stays locked away
An emptiness in my soul
Never seeing light of day

A part of me that is broken
Always longing to connect
I must keep it forever hidden
So, no one can detect

Full of darkness and sorrow
An intensity that overwhelms
Best to keep under control
Better versions at the helm

It is ever present
Heaviness weighing me down
Whispering to me of its longing
To finally be found

Reality

Life seems a series
Of both consequence and fate
Choices confined
Each carries a weight

Some weigh more heavily
Becoming burdens to bare
Destiny plays its role
Trapped in life's lair

Still we hold out hope
Believing we are free
Swallowing the blue pill
Into a veiled reality

Bound

The void looms large
Obscuring my view
Emptiness overwhelms
Sadness overdue

Barriers to connection
Familiar and profound
Back to where I began
In silence I am bound

Loneliness like no other
Such salient parts of me
Ever present and entrenched
For this is all I will ever be

Solitude becomes a gift
Comforting in its embrace
Withdrawing into myself
So only the mirror I face

Being

I am neither broken nor lost
Just intense at a cost
A steep price to pay
For in the abyss I stay

Because so few can manage
The pressure and depth
I am mostly alone
In darkness and death

A place where thoughts cannot escape
Nor do they decay
Water so heavy and still
They do not float away

This heaviness of life
Takes its toll
But here I find comfort
An anchoring of my soul

Never-Ending Story

There is no escape
From this cycle of pain
Where darkness and shadows
And demons reign

Over and over
Battles are fought
Trenches appear
Scarring the heart

Soul grows weary
Barriers in place
Cycle continues
Losing the race

Walls crumble
Reality floods in
Pulling me under
Drowning again

Fighting to the surface
Drawing last breath
Weight of existence
Dragging me to my death

Dust In The Wind

What is left of the soul
After life takes its toll
The molding of clay
Then chipping away

Illusion of time
Binds us sublime
Traps us in space
Running in place

Then leaves us bereft
A painful, shattering theft
Many pieces are lost
At such a steep cost

Life continues on
Until all fragments are gone
Then the toll has been paid
And into dust, we all fade.

Sound Of Silence

The sound of silence
Pure and true
A peaceful stillness
Through and through

In that stillness
Mystery abounds
Freedom from chains
Weighing me down

Life incognito
Dark and alone
Sound of silence
Calling me home

Journey

Life is for the living
Those who can carry the weight
The cumulative experience
Of both free will and fate

Chapter after chapter
An epic novel slowly born
Outlining the details
Of a life weathered and worn

Both spellbinding and average
Life eventually takes its toll
Accumulation of choices
Weigh heavy on the soul

Often the weight a burden
Reality a fusion of time
An arrow seeking a target
Past is prologue to what it will find

A journey to a destination
An intricate tapestry weaved
Only in death the burden lifted
Life's lesson finally received

Quicksand

Resistance is futile
Or so it seems
Lost in the void
Of rabid themes

Feckless and hollow
World gone mad
Loudest voices
Latest fad

So tired of fighting
For what seems right
Forever resisting
Cultural blight

For something of meaning
And for something that's fair
Existential purpose
For which the world doesn't care

Weight Of The World

Weight of the world
Pulling me down
Will to go on
Both lost and found

There seems no escape
From this prison of mind
No peace or comfort
No solace to find

Drowning in chaos
No one can see
Voices so heavy
Will not let me be

The longing for silence
A safe space to hide
Exhausted from swimming
Against the tide

The Wall

I know that my life
Is not what it seems
The external facade
All masks and schemes

Necessity at times
Play by their rules
Leaving me empty
Like ghosts and ghouls

If only to be able
To really be me
But hiding away
Seems my destiny

For no one can handle
The loneliness and pain
The depth of me
Both strength and bane

So I must hide away
Behind the wall
Carefully constructed
Never to fall

Timeless

There is a synergy, an essence
To all that is
An interconnectedness of space and time
Life takes, and it gives

Perhaps it is the pursuit of balance
Ever Nature's plan
Seasons change bringing perspective
Understanding the place of man

Arrow of time moves onward
A complex tapestry weaved
The fragility and nuance of life
For the observer and perceived

Both beautiful and brutal
Building up and tearing down
Recycling of the elements
Into the mundane and the profound

Perhaps the mysteries of the universe
And all the realities within
Just possibilities of chance and mathematics
Wrapped in illusion of choice and original sin

In Hiding

Pain strikes without warning
Shocking the system anew
Burden of life weighs heavy
Reality of what is true

An overwhelming despair
Seeded by loneliness and doubt
A darkness slowly descends
Turning me inside out

Then as the puzzle pieces of me
Unlock and start to fray
A facade so carefully constructed
Begins to crumble away

What remains is so absolute and intense
It has nowhere to go
Keeping it hidden away
So no one can ever know

Afterword

All these poems are expressions of my search for meaning in a world that is increasingly chaotic, maddening and obtrusive. I have learned so much about myself and others through this process. I now better understand my inability to connect, my categorical and black and white thinking, my strong moral code and loyalty, my strong connection to animals and the environment, my need for respite and retreat and my struggles with a society that increasingly seems vacuous and shallow. Social media has infiltrated our lives in ways that we all know are unhealthy and addictive. Science and technology have increasingly moved forward at a pace that is beyond our ability to keep up. Global climate change has worsened (as predicted) and we have become more nationalistic and cruel because of it. I have a theory that if these patterns hold, we will only become "meaner", greedier and more selfish as resources become scarcer, AI and robotics begin to take over jobs and we begin to experience the true impacts of what we have brought on ourselves. Deep down, we all know this is coming and will only get worse. How we navigate this will be the true measure of our humanity. I will continue to write to try to find a way to express both to myself and the world – how someone with ASD, who often does see the patterns long before others, is processing such change, in the midst of searching for the real me. I fear the turbulence will be overwhelming and my only respite may be to withdraw and disengage. We will see.